Love that Changes SADNESS to JOY

Archway Publishing books may be ordered through booksellers or by contacting:

Archway Publishing
1663 Liberty Drive
Bloomington, IN 47403
www.archwaypublishing.com
844-669-3957

• Scripture quotations are from New Revised Standard Version Bible, copyright © 1989 National Council of the Churches of Christ in the United States of America. Used by permission. All rights reserved worldwide.

ISBN: 978-1-6657-1061-9 (sc)
ISBN: 978-1-6657-1062-6 (hc)
ISBN: 978-1-6657-1063-3 (e)

Print information available on the last page.

Archway Publishing rev. date: 08/18/2021

Love

that changes

SADNESS to JOY

SHIRLEY R. SMITH

My name is Sydney.

I am 4 years old.

I want to tell you my story.

The story that changed my sadness into joy.

My Daddy died in January from the Covid 19 virus.

He was a paramedic.

A first responder.

A hero.

My Mommy always worked to help Daddy with the family income.

She used to love her job, bouncing out of bed each morning, preparing breakfast and to-go lunches for all three of us.

She hummed a favorite tune as we walked to the car each morning.

Driving me to school her face was sunny even on the gloomiest day.

I could see that getting out of bed for Mommy was not so easy anymore.

She followed our routine out of habit.

Her sadness was like mine, but larger.

She had to be a parent while carrying around the heavy heart we shared.

I have a babysitter named Cathy, a student at Bucknell University.

She has been my sitter after school since I was three.

Normally, I would talk Cathy's ear off with anything and everything from my day.

Now, my sadness left me with no words to share.

Poor Cathy. Playtime and hot chocolate could not stop my tears or get me to open up.

Mommy and I tried to comfort each other each evening after her long day of work. Our hearts, though, were just not ready to feel better.

Mommy was sitting in the living room one evening when her eyes fell on the old piano across the room.

She decided to ask me if I would like to take some piano lessons.

She thought something new in my life might cheer me up.

I liked music. I sang around the house all the time. Well, I did. (Sigh.)

I would sing "This Little Light of Mine"

"Down in My Heart"

"All Things Bright and Beautiful"

"I'm Gonna Sing When the Spirit Says Sing"

so loud that passersby could hear me.

That weekend, I met the teacher mommy had in mind. She was like a grandmother----gentle, kind, understanding, and a good listener.

In time I began to share with her my feelings of loss and my concerns for my mommy.

I could feel my heart awaken again to life through music.

I practiced every day and became one of Mrs. Smith's best students.

Now, Mrs. Smith was the choir director at the Community Presbyterian Church in town.

One day she asked me if I would like to join the children's choir at the church.

I was thrilled and mommy gave her approval readily.

The choir sang once a month and Mommy was always in the first pew to listen.

I loved showing her the joy I had found through music and a heart that was beginning to feel lighter.

On the Sundays that the choir sang I also attended Sunday School where I learned such amazing stories about this man called Jesus and His father, God.

We memorized wonderful verses like,

"I can do all things through Christ" (Phil 4:13)

"Trust in the Lord with all your heart" (Prov 3:5)

"Do not fear for I am with you" (Isa 41:10)

"I give you a new commandment that you love one another" (Jn 13:34) AND

"We love because He first loved us." (1 Jn 4: 19)

Did He and His Father really love me no matter what I did?

Did he understand why I shut out the joys in this life after Daddy died?

Of course, He did.

I prayed for His forgiveness but as I did, I knew I was already forgiven.

The joy showered upon me the day I first believed was like a gentle rain on a sunny afternoon.

The warmth of His love is forever.

Now 5 years old, I found myself doing anything and everything I could to help with projects at church.

I collected food for the hungry, helped to raise money for turkeys to be given to families at Thanksgiving, and gathered gifts for the homeless children at Christmas.

My joy was almost complete, even on the days that I expected Daddy to walk in the door after work. And he did not.

And, of course, I still worried about Mommy.

That Christmas Eve the miracle for which I had waited so long happened.

Mommy attended the Christmas Eve service in which I was not just any angel but the Angel Gabriel.

At the end of the pageant, I came before the entire cast of characters and proclaimed with arms stretched out and raised to the heavens that,

Jesus is Born.

He is our Savior.

He is our Future.

He is our Father, husband, son, brother, and Comforter.

A Blessed Christmas to all!

The congregation was on their feet with applause and tears of joy as they began singing.

Joy to the World the Lord is come!

Let earth receive her King;

Let every heart prepare Him room

And heaven and nature sing.

Mommy, with tears streaming down her face, threw her arms around me.

She had witnessed the re-creation of her daughter.

Led by the children that night, she had caught that contagious joy so impossible to resist.

She became a believer in the power of Jesus' love that very night.

She now knew that God would see them through anything.

She saw the light of that Christmas star looming large before them and knew that it would light their way forever.

The End

Printed in the United States
by Baker & Taylor Publisher Services